CAUSE AND EFFECT

Freedom FROM SLAVERY

CAUSES AND EFFECTS

of the **Emancipation Proclamation**

BY BRIANNA HALL

Consultant:
Malcolm J. Rohrbough
Professor Emeritus
Department of History
The University of Iowa
Iowa City, Iowa

CAPSTONE PRESS
a capstone imprint

T0051066

Fact Finders Books are published by Capstone Press,
1710 Roe Crest Drive, North Mankato, Minnesota 56003
www.capstonepub.com

Library of Congress Cataloging-in-Publication Data
Cataloging-in-publication information is on file with the Library of Congress.
ISBN: 978-1-4765-3930-0 (library binding)
ISBN: 978-1-4765-5128-9 (paperback)
ISBN: 978-1-4765-5977-3 (eBook PDF)

Editorial Credits
Abby Colich, editor; Kyle Grenz, designer; Svetlana Zhurkin, media researcher;
Jennifer Walker, production specialist

Photo Credits
Alamy: North Wind Picture Archives, cover (middle), 4, 11, 28; Library of Congress,
cover (inset), 12, 14, 15, 17, 18, 20, 25, 27; National Park Service: Harpers Ferry Center/
Keith Rocco, 23, Colonial National Historical Park/Sidney E. King, 7; Shutterstock:
Christopher Parypa, 29

Table OF CONTENTS

Slavery in America

Slavery was common in early America. Owning a black person in 1750 seemed no different than owning a horse. Farmers owned slaves who worked in their fields. Merchants owned slaves who worked in their homes. Even America's early leaders who fought for independence owned slaves.

Rich **plantation** owners wanted slaves to help them make money quickly. Lawmakers in southern states passed laws to keep slavery legal. Their states benefited from using slaves.

Slaves greet their owners outside their cabins in Virginia in the 1700s.

Abolitionists worked hard to end slavery. The first abolitionists were religious groups called Quakers and Puritans. They believed in freedom for all. Freed slaves often became abolitionists too. They experienced firsthand the pain of being a slave. Some lawmakers joined the abolitionists. To abolitionists, the U.S. Constitution granted freedom to all.

Conflicts escalated between lawmakers, abolitionists, and Southern slave holders. As a result, the United States entered a civil war. The introduction of the Emancipation Proclamation in 1863 led to a new era of freedom.

plantation—a large farm found in warm areas; before the Civil War, plantations in the South used slave labor
abolitionist—a person who worked to end slavery

What Caused the EMANCIPATION PROCLAMATION?

President Abraham Lincoln announced the Emancipation Proclamation on September 22, 1862. The Proclamation stated that about 3.5 million slaves in Confederate states would be free beginning January 1, 1863.

Cause #1: Europeans Settle in America

Europeans arrived in North America in the 1600s. Some of the settlers brought African slaves with them. These **colonists** saw the chance to make money in the vast farmlands. They built big plantations using slave labor.

colonist—a person who settles in a new territory that is governed by his or her home country, the settled area is called a colony

Early colonists build a fort at Jamestown, Virginia, in 1607.

At the time, Great Britain owned the American colonies. Colonists followed British laws and paid British taxes. Eventually colonists no longer wanted to live under Great Britain's rule. They fought to become a new nation. In 1776 patriots signed the Declaration of Independence, and the United States of America was formed. Slavery remained a part of American life.

Cause #2: The Slave Trade

The slave trade was a successful business in the United States. Merchants began in New England with ships full of American goods such as timber and cotton. Next they sailed across the Atlantic Ocean to trade these goods with African leaders. In return for the timber and cotton, merchants were given shackled slaves. This practice became known as the "triangle trade."

The most dangerous part of the journey followed. Called the Middle Passage, this area stretched between Africa and the West Indies. Up to half of all slaves died from disease or starvation while crossing the Middle Passage.

FAST FACT: The exact number of African people shipped across the Middle Passage is unknown. Researchers estimate that 10 million to 12 million Africans were transported between the 1600s and the 1800s.

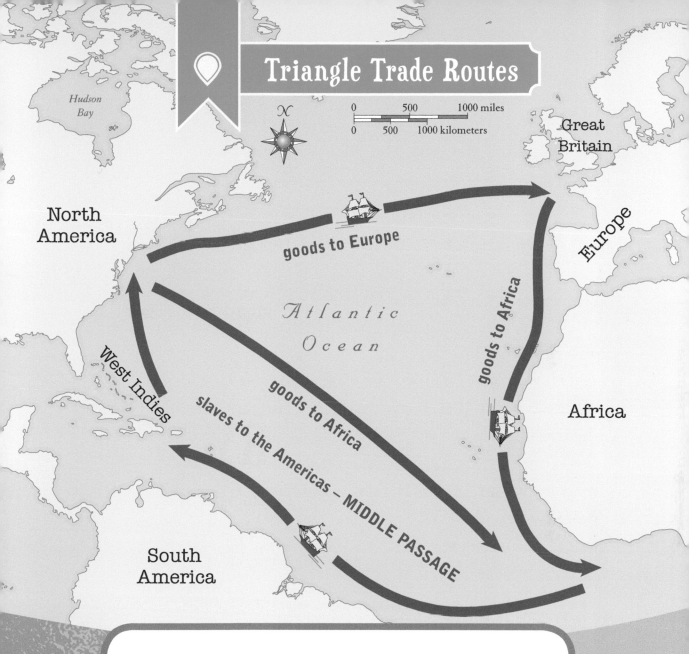

Triangle Trade Routes

Hudson
Bay

Great
Britain

North
America

goods to Europe

Europe

Atlantic
Ocean

goods to Africa

West Indies

goods to Africa

slaves to the Americas – MIDDLE PASSAGE

Africa

South
America

When slaves reached the West Indies, settlers traded them for molasses and sugar. They came to North America in the final part of the trip. There North Americans bought the African men, women, and children at slave auctions.

Cause #3: Northern States Ban Slavery

The invention of machines that spun cotton into yarn sparked the American **Industrial Revolution** (1790–1860). Factories sprang up in northern states. For the first time, companies used power made by animals, steam, and water to create goods. There was less of a need for slaves in the northern states.

Northern states decided to ban slavery. Vermont **abolished** slavery first in 1777. Massachusetts followed in 1783. Eventually, every northern state passed anti-slavery laws.

However, the demand for slaves remained high in southern states. Slaves were even more important after the invention of the cotton gin. This machine removed seeds from cotton 50 times faster than by hand. The machine's speed meant plantation owners could grow more cotton. Harvesting still needed to be done by hand, so growers kept slaves working in the fields.

Industrial Revolution—a period from 1790 to 1860 when work began to be done by machines, rather than by hand
abolish—to put an end to something officially

Cotton was an important crop in the South. Plantation owners depended on slaves to do the harvesting.

Cause #4: Growing Tensions Between the North and South

Lawmakers tried to talk with one another to solve growing tensions between Northern and Southern states. Southern leaders were upset because they did not have as many votes in Congress as the Northern states. Fewer votes could mean the end of slavery in the South.

In 1820 the United States had 22 states. Eleven states were slave states, and 11 were free states. As new states joined the United States, neither the North nor the South wanted to lose power in Congress. So Congress created the Missouri Compromise Line. Land north of the line became free land, with the exception of Missouri. Land south of the line allowed slavery.

This compromise only solved problems for a short period of time. In the long run, the North and South grew further apart.

Abraham Lincoln was sworn in as U.S. president on March 4, 1861. Southerners did not like his views on slavery.

Union and Confederate Populations

In the 1860 census, nearly 4 million slaves lived in the United States (3,953,760 people, to be exact).

people in millions

25
20
15
10
5
0

Slaves
White
Military-aged men

South   North

Cause #5: Secession

In 1860 disagreements exploded between Northern and Southern states. Southern leaders were angry with the U.S. government. They believed each state had the right to make its own decision about slavery.

Slave owners feared the government would get rid of slavery. Without slaves, plantation owners might lose their money, land, and power. Even non-slave owning southern whites did not trust the North and its anti-slavery ideas.

Lincoln's presidential victory in 1860 angered southerners even more. South Carolina **seceded** from the United States first. Over the next six weeks, six more states left the **Union**. By February 1861, the 11 states that seceded created a constitution. Jefferson Davis was elected president of the Confederate States of America.

secede—to formally withdraw from a group or an organization, often to form another organization

Union—the United States of America; also the Northern states that fought against the Southern states in the Civil War

Cause #6: The Civil War

The Civil War began in April 1861. Both the **Confederacy** and Union thought their own side would win quickly. But the war dragged on for four years. An estimated 620,000 soldiers lost their lives.

Soldiers, lawmakers, and citizens supported the war for different reasons. Confederates defended the right for each state to make its own laws. They wanted to continue slavery and plantation life. Northern states, known as the Union, wanted the United States to stay as one country. Some Union soldiers fought to end slavery.

Union and Confederate troops at the Battle of Antietam, September 17, 1862

Confederacy—the Southern states that fought against the Northern states in the Civil War; also called the Confederate States of America

Battle of Fort Sumter: Beginning of the American Civil War

The Battle at Fort Sumter was Lincoln's first big test as president. South Carolina demanded that Union soldiers empty their buildings within the Confederacy. Lincoln had to choose to defend his forts or allow Confederate soldiers to capture them. Lincoln and Major Robert Anderson chose not to surrender Fort Sumter without a battle. Confederate troops bombarded the fort in the early morning of April 12, 1861. Union soldiers were outnumbered. They battled for two days before surrendering. Even though he lost, the battle at Fort Sumter sent a message to the Confederacy. The Union was willing to fight.

THE *Emancipation* PROCLAMATION

President Lincoln wrote the Emancipation Proclamation during the summer of 1862. Americans had been fighting each other for more than a year. Lincoln was trying to end the war and reunite the country. At first no one knew about the Emancipation Proclamation except his cabinet members.

Lincoln waited for a Union military victory to share his plan with Congress. He got his chance in September 1862 after the bloody battle of Antietam in Maryland. The announcement gave the 10 rebel states a choice. If they rejoined the Union, slavery would remain legal in the south. If they did not rejoin the Union, slaves would be freed. None of the Confederate states rejoined the Union. Lincoln followed through with his warning. He signed the Emancipation Proclamation into law on January 1, 1863.

"…all persons held as slaves within any State or designated part of a State, the people whereof shall then be in rebellion against the United States, shall be then, thenceforward, and forever free…"

PROCLAMATION OF EMANCIPATION

1861 — 1863

By the President of the United States of America.

Whereas, On the Twenty-Second day of September, in the year of our Lord one thousand eight hundred and sixty-two, a Proclamation was issued by the President of the United States, containing, among other things the following, to wit:

"That on the first day of January, in the year of our Lord one thousand eight hundred and sixty-three, all persons held as slaves within any State or designated part of a State, the people whereof shall then be in rebellion against the United States, shall be then, thenceforth, and **FOREVER FREE**, and the **EXECUTIVE GOVERNMENT OF THE UNITED STATES,** including the military and naval authorities thereof, **WILL RECOGNIZE AND MAINTAIN THE FREEDOM** of such persons, and will do no act or acts to repress such persons, or any of them, in any efforts they may make for their actual freedom.

"That the Executive will, on the first day of January aforesaid, by proclamation, designate the States and parts of States, if any, in which the people thereof respectively shall then be in rebellion against the United States, and the fact that any State, or the people thereof shall on that day be in good faith represented in the Congress of the United States by members chosen thereto at elections wherein a majority of the qualified voters of such State shall have participated, shall, in the absence of strong countervailing testimony be deemed conclusive evidence that such State and the people thereof are not then in rebellion against the United States."

Now, therefore, I, ABRAHAM LINCOLN, PRESIDENT OF THE UNITED STATES, by virtue of the power in me vested as Commander-in-Chief of the Army and Navy of the United States in time of actual armed Rebellion against the authority and government of the United States, and as a fit and necessary war measure for suppressing said Rebellion, do, on this first day of January, in the year of our Lord one thousand eight hundred and sixty-three, and in accordance with my purpose so to do, publicly proclaim for the full period of one hundred days from the day of the first above-mentioned order, and designate, as the States and parts of States wherein the people thereof respectively are this day in rebellion against the United States, the following, to wit: ARKANSAS, TEXAS, LOUISIANA (except the Parishes of St. Bernard, Plaquemines, Jefferson, St. John, St. Charles, St. James, Ascension, Assumption, Terre Bonne, La Fourche, St. Mary, St. Martin, and Orleans, including the City of Orleans), MISSISSIPPI, ALABAMA, FLORIDA, GEORGIA, SOUTH CAROLINA, NORTH CAROLINA, AND VIRGINIA (except the forty-eight counties designated as West Virginia, and also the counties of Berkeley, Accomac, Northampton, Elizabeth City, York, Princess Ann, and Norfolk, including the cities of Norfolk and Portsmouth), and which excepted parts are for the present left precisely as if this Proclamation were not issued.

And by virtue of the power and for the purpose aforesaid, I do order and declare that **ALL PERSONS HELD AS SLAVES** within said designated States and parts of States are, AND HENCEFORWARD **SHALL BE FREE!** and that the Executive Government of the United States, including the Military and Naval Authorities thereof, will **RECOGNIZE AND MAINTAIN THE FREEDOM** of said persons.

And I hereby enjoin upon the people so declared to be free, to abstain from all violence, UNLESS IN NECESSARY SELF-DEFENCE, and I recommend to them that in all cases, when allowed, they **LABOR FAITHFULLY FOR REASONABLE WAGES.**

And I further declare and make known that such persons of suitable condition will be received into the armed service of the United States, to garrison forts, positions, stations, and other places, and to man vessels of all sorts in said service.

And upon this act, **SINCERELY BELIEVED TO BE AN ACT OF JUSTICE,** warranted by the Constitution, upon military necessity, I invoke the considerate judgment of mankind, and the gracious favor of ALMIGHTY GOD.

In testimony whereof I have hereunto set my name, and caused the seal of the United States to be affixed.

[L. S.]

Done at the City of Washington, this first day of January, in the year of our Lord one thousand eight hundred and sixty-three, and of the Independence of the United States the eighty-seventh.

A. Lincoln

By the President.
William H. Seward
Secretary of State.

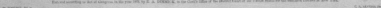

Entered according to Act of Congress, in the year 1864 by E. A. DIMMICK, in the Clerk's Office of the District Court of the United States for the Southern District of New York.

Impact

Only a small number of slaves in Confederate states were freed right away. More were freed as Union soldiers took over Confederate areas. The Emancipation Proclamation didn't free slaves in the four border states that were still a part of the Union. Freedom for all slaves in the United States wouldn't come until later.

African-American Union soldiers

FAST FACT: Nearly 200,000 freed slaves fought for the Union in the Civil War.

CONFEDERATE STATES

UNION STATES

BORDER STATES

Lincoln believed that slavery should be abolished. But by issuing the Emancipation Proclamation, he was also trying to do something else. He knew that without slaves to do work, the Confederacy would weaken. He wanted the Confederate states to surrender and the Civil War to end. The Emancipation Proclamation also said that freed slaves could join the Union Army. The additional soldiers would make the Union army stronger.

Until now, Lincoln's main goal for winning the war was to reunite the North and South. The Emancipation Proclamation made ending slavery a main purpose of the war.

The Response

The Emancipation Proclamation was an important move. A president had never made such a big decision without Congress. Some legislators, Unionists, and Confederates thought Lincoln had abused his power. They argued the Emancipation Proclamation was illegal.

The Constitution says that a president is "Commander in Chief of the Army and Navy." Lincoln said that this gave him the authority to issue the Emancipation Proclamation. But many people still thought that Lincoln didn't have the right to declare slaves in Southern states freed. This belief made ending the war and passing a law to free slaves very important to Lincoln.

Even people in the Union disliked Lincoln's announcement. High-ranking Union officer General George McClellan urged Lincoln to keep emancipation out of the war. Many people from northern states fought to preserve the Union. They did not care about ending slavery. Angry Unionists retaliated by attacking and killing black people during the summer of 1863. They attacked abolitionists too.

Some freed slaves after the issue of the Emancipation Proclamation leave their plantation in North Carolina.

The Effects of the EMANCIPATION PROCLAMATION

The Emancipation Proclamation began the process to end slavery in the United States. While the document began important changes, the struggle for African-American freedom was only beginning.

Effect #1: Surrender of the Confederacy

The Emancipation Proclamation weakened the South. The military needed slaves to provide food and supplies. By 1865 many Confederate soldiers left the army.

FAST FACT: More than 360,000 Union soldiers died in the Civil War. Another 258,000 Confederate soldiers died. Disease spread through the camps and killed more soldiers than battle.

Confederate General Robert E. Lee surrenders to Union General Ulysses S. Grant in Appomattox, Virginia.

The Confederacy experienced growing chaos. Many plantation owners lost everything overnight. Union troops stole their crops, killed their livestock, and burned their homes. They freed slaves as they marched toward the Confederate capital in Richmond, Virginia. Union soldiers entered the capital on April 3, 1865. At that time, Union troops outnumbered the Confederates two to one. Five days later, the Confederate army surrendered. The Civil War was over.

Effect #2: The 13th Amendment

The 13th **Amendment** finished what the Emancipation Proclamation had started. It ended slavery in the United States forever.

Lincoln offered the amendment to Congress in September 1862 before he announced the Emancipation Proclamation. The amendment received the needed votes in the Senate but could not pass in the House of Representatives.

Lincoln worked hard to pass the amendment. He published letters in newspapers to gain public support. He visited lawmakers to convince them. Against all odds, the 13th Amendment passed in the House of Representatives on January 31, 1865.

FAST FACT: Amending the Constitution is difficult. Lincoln's slavery amendment took nearly three years to get enough votes.

amendment—a change made to a law or a legal document
ratify—to officially approve something

Sadly, Lincoln never saw the amendment officially added to the Constitution. John Wilkes Booth killed him on April 15, 1865, eight months before it was **ratified**.

The 14th and 15th Amendments to the Constitution followed in 1868 and 1870. The 14th Amendment granted citizenship to former slaves. The 15th Amendment gave black men the right to vote.

Representatives cheer at the passing of the 13th Amendment.

Effect #3: On the Move

Life for former slaves did not improve much after the war. Rich, white men still owned most of the land and buildings. They forced families to live in broken-down shacks. Black people rented part of the land in a system called **sharecropping**. They farmed the land, but landowners made sure the families never made any money. They charged unfair rent and did not allow blacks to keep the harvests. Children worked in the fields and rarely had the chance to attend school.

Cities to the north and west offered new jobs and new lives. Many freed slaves moved from rural farmlands in the south to large cities in the north. Black populations of cities like Washington, D.C., New York, and Chicago quickly grew.

Effect #4: Civil Rights Movement

In the 1960s nearly everything in the south was **segregated** by race. Blacks could not attend the same schools as white people. They could not live in the same neighborhoods or use the same drinking fountains. In the south, many black people could not vote. **Jim Crow laws** made this **discrimination** legal.

sharecropping—farming a piece of land and paying the owner of the land with money from the crops raised
segregate—to keep people of different races apart in schools and other public places
Jim Crow laws—laws saying that that African-Americans and European Americans should live separately but equally
discrimination—treating people unfairly because of their race, country of birth, or gender

Black and white people march together for civil rights in Alabama in 1965.

African-American communities organized to create change. They believed everyone deserved the same rights and demanded equality.

Dr. Martin Luther King Jr. became a leader of nonviolent protests. He organized rallies, made speeches, and wrote letters. It was difficult and dangerous work. In 1968 Dr. Martin Luther King Jr. was murdered.

Slowly, the U.S. government ended the Jim Crow laws. The Civil Rights Act of 1964 stopped segregation in schools and public places. The Voting Rights Act of 1965 supported the 15th Amendment by ending voter discrimination laws.

Cause and Effect—A Changed Nation

Lincoln wanted to abolish slavery in the United States. Although not all slaves were freed until after the Civil War, the Emancipation Proclamation changed the nation. It helped lead to a Union victory in the war. After the war the 13th Amendment guaranteed freedom from slavery in the United States, a path paved by the Emancipation Proclamation.

African-Americans celebrate the end of slavery in Washington, D.C., in 1866.

African-Americans continue to celebrate their progress, including Barack Obama's first day as president in 2009.

Life was not easy for freed slaves. They lived in poor conditions and worked as sharecroppers. They suffered discrimination. African-American families began moving north to find better opportunities. Many people worked together to help African-Americans get equal rights in the United States.

By signing the Emancipation Proclamation, Lincoln signaled a turning point in the Civil War. The proclamation forced the nation to address the issue of slavery and equal rights for all.

GLOSSARY

abolish (uh-BOL-ish)—to put an end to something officially

abolitionist (ab-uh-LI-shuhn-ist)—a person who worked to end slavery

amendment (uh-MEND-muhnt)—a change made to a law or a legal document

colonist (KAH-luh-nist)—a person who settles in a new territory that is governed by his or her home country, the settled area is called a colony

Confederacy (kuhn-FE-druh-see)—the Southern states that fought against the Northern states in the Civil War; also called the Confederate States of America

discrimination (dis-kri-muh-NAY-shuhn)—treating people unfairly because of their race, country of birth, or gender

Industrial Revolution (in-DUHSS-tree-uhl rev-uh-LOO-shuhn)—a period from 1790 to 1860 when work began to be done by machines, rather than by hand

Jim Crow laws (JIM KROH LAWZ)—laws saying that that African-Americans and European Americans should live separately but equally

plantation (plan-TAY-shuhn)—a large farm found in warm areas; before the Civil War, plantations in the South used slave labor

ratify (RA-ti-fye)—to officially approve something

secede (si-SEED)—to formally withdraw from a group or an organization, often to form another organization

segregate (SEG-ruh-gate)—to keep people of different races apart in schools and other public places

sharecropping (SHAIR-krop-ing)—farming a piece of land and paying the owner of the land with money from the crops raised

Union (YOON-yuhn)—the United States of America; also the Northern states that fought against the Southern states in the Civil War

READ MORE

Bolden, Tonya. *Emancipation Proclamation: Lincoln and the Dawn of Liberty.* New York: Abrams Books for Young Readers, 2013.

Clark, Willow. *The True Story of the Emancipation Proclamation.* What Really Happened? New York: PowerKids Press, 2013

Landau, Elaine. *The Emancipation Proclamation: Would You Do What Lincoln Did?* What Would You Do? Berkeley Heights, N.J.: Enslow Elementary, 2008.

Yomtov, Nel. *True Stories of the Civil War.* Stories of War. North Mankato, Minn.: Capstone Press, 2013.

INTERNET SITES

FactHound offers a safe, fun way to find Internet sites related to this book. All of the sites on FactHound have been researched by our staff.

Here's all you do:

Visit *www.facthound.com*

Type in this code: 9781476539300

Check out projects, games and lots more at
www.capstonekids.com

CRITICAL THINKING USING THE COMMON CORE

1. Examine the bar graph on page 12. How do you think the slave and white populations of the North and South affected the outcome of the Civil War? What else do you think it affected? (Craft and Structure)

2. Suppose that Abraham Lincoln had not issued the Emancipation Proclamation. How might the Civil War turned out differently? What else would be different today? (Integration of Knowledge and Ideas)

3. How do you think Southerners responded to losing the Civil War? Use details from the text to support your answer. (Key Idea and Details)

INDEX